DO NOT INFLATE
※※ AS THIS MAY IMPEDE YOUR EXIT ※※
DED ASSOCIATES

LAURENCE KING

LEGAL
PUBLISHED IN 2002 BY LAURENCE KING PUBLISHING
71 GREAT RUSSELL STREET
LONDON WC1B 3BP
TEL: +44 020 7430 8850
FAX: +44 020 7430 8880
E-MAIL: ENQUIRIES@LAURENCEKING.CO.UK
WWW.LAURENCEKING.CO.UK

COPYRIGHT © 2002 DED ASSOCIATES LIMITED
E-MAIL: DNI@DEDASS.COM WWW.DEDASS.COM WWW.BUYDED.COM

ALL RIGHTS RESERVED. NO PART OF THIS PUBLICATION MAY BE REPRODUCED OR
TRANSMITTED IN ANY FORM OR BY ANY MEANS, ELECTRONIC OR MECHANICAL,
INCLUDING PHOTOCOPY, RECORDING OR ANY INFORMATION STORAGE AND RETRIEVAL SYSTEM,
WITHOUT PERMISSION IN WRITING FROM THE PUBLISHER.

A CATALOGUE RECORD FOR THIS BOOK IS AVAILABLE FROM THE BRITISH LIBRARY.
ISBN 1 85669 248 5

WITHDRAWN

NORTHAMPTON COLLEGE

R54475M0098

FOREWORD

BUCKLE UP, CHECK THE VIEW OUT OF THE WINDOW AND UNWRAP A BOILED SWEET. IN THIS AGE OF PACKAGE HOLIDAYS AND INTERNATIONAL BUSINESS, WE'RE ALL SEASONED TRAVELLERS AND WE'VE SEEN THE DRILL DOZENS OF TIMES. ALL WE WANT TO KNOW IS WHERE THE NEAREST DOOR IS.

THERE ARE REASONS WHY WE LEAVE THE SAFETY CARD TUCKED INTO THE ELASTICATED POCKET IN FRONT (PREFERABLY TOTALLY HIDDEN FROM VIEW BY THE IN-FLIGHT MAGAZINE). NO MATTER HOW MANY TIMES YOU FLY, THERE REMAINS AN EXPECTATION OF GLAMOUR ABOUT THE EXPERIENCE. THE BIG OPERATORS, ENGAGED IN A DOGFIGHT FOR OUR AIR MILES, LIKE TO SUSTAIN THE ILLUSION. JUST LOOK AT THEIR TV ADS FOR THE PROMISES THEY MAKE: BEAUTIFUL, COMPLIANT STEWARDESSES, FOUR-STAR FOOD, CLOUDLESS SKIES AND EVERY SIGN THAT YOU'RE THE ONLY PASSENGER ON BOARD. COMPARE IT WITH THE REALITY: THE ORANGE, DISINTERESTED ATTENDANTS; THE PRESSURISED, DEHUMIDIFIED AIR; THE INDIGESTIBLE IN-FLIGHT MEAL; THE THREAT FROM CRAMPED SEATS OF DEEP-VEIN THROMBOSIS; THE SICK BAG; THE SAFETY CARD. WHEN YOU STEP ON A PLANE, YOU'RE STEPPING INTO A SYSTEM WHERE YOUR IDENTITY IS STOWED AWAY WITH YOUR LUGGAGE. YOU'RE ASKED TO CONFORM TO A CERTAIN SIZE, SHAPE, APPETITE AND SET OF MANNERS. PEOPLE DON'T LIKE THAT. OCCASIONALLY, THEY LOSE THEIR HEADS AND BECOME VIOLENT. SOMETIMES THEY REACT IN QUITE UNEXPECTED WAYS: THE FIRST CLASS PASSENGER WHO DEFECATED ON THE FOOD TROLLEY, FOR EXAMPLE, OR THE ACIDHEAD WHO TRIED TO BLESS THE COCKPIT CREW. WHILE THE REST OF THE WORLD IS URGING YOU TO EXPRESS YOUR INDIVIDUALITY, AIRLINES INSIST YOU ADOPT A DIFFERENT, LESS TROUBLESOME MODEL. IT'S THE FLAT, CHARACTERLESS AUTOMATON ON THE SAFETY CARD.

NO-ONE'S INTERESTED, AND IT'S NOT SURPRISING: WHO IS GOING TO BEHAVE LIKE A FIGURE FROM A 1960S DIY MANUAL, EVEN IF IT IS JUST FOR A COUPLE OF HOURS? IF ANYONE ACTUALLY DID, IT WOULD EITHER BE FUNNY OR FRIGHTENING. AS FRIGHTENING AS, SAY, A SUDDEN LOSS OF ALTITUDE. OR A LOUD THUD FROM ONE OF THE WINGS. WHICH LEADS US FINALLY TO THE DARK PLACE FROM WHICH OUR DISQUIET WITH SAFETY CARDS REALLY STEMS. LIKE THE BEST HORROR MOVIES, IT'S WHAT THE CARDS LEAVE OUT OF THE SITUATIONS THEY DEPICT THAT AFFECTS US MOST STRONGLY. DESIGNED TO REASSURE US, THEIR SANITISED LINE DRAWINGS AND PERFECTLY EXECUTED EXIT MANOEUVRES SIMPLY INVITE OUR IMAGINATIONS TO SILENTLY RUN RIOT. WE SEE THE SILHOUETTED PLANE THAT'S ABOUT TO DITCH IN THE SEA AND IMAGINE LOTS OF TINY BLACK BITS FLOATING ON THE SURFACE A FEW MOMENTS LATER. WE SEE THE ROW OF PASSENGERS IN THE BRACE POSITION AND WONDER WHICH ONE'S GOING TO BE LUCKY. WE SEE THE SMILING WOMAN TYING HER LIFE JACKET AND PICTURE A CABIN FULL OF SCREAMING PEOPLE BEHIND HER.

LIKE HORROR MOVIES, AIRLINE SAFETY CARDS CAN SCARE THE WITS OUT OF US. BUT REALLY THEY ARE ENTERTAINMENT. REST ASSURED, IT'LL (PROBABLY) NEVER HAPPEN TO YOU.

THE BOOK IS THE WORK OF DESIGN DECONSTRUCTIVISTS AND SAFETY CARD FETISHISTS ▇▇▇ ▇▇▇ ▇▇▇ AND IS A HYMN TO THE ON BOARD SAFETY CARD. EXTINGUISH ALL CIGARETTES, STRAP YOURSELF IN WITH A MICROWAVEABLE DINNER AND DO NOT INFLATE.

MICHAEL EVAMY

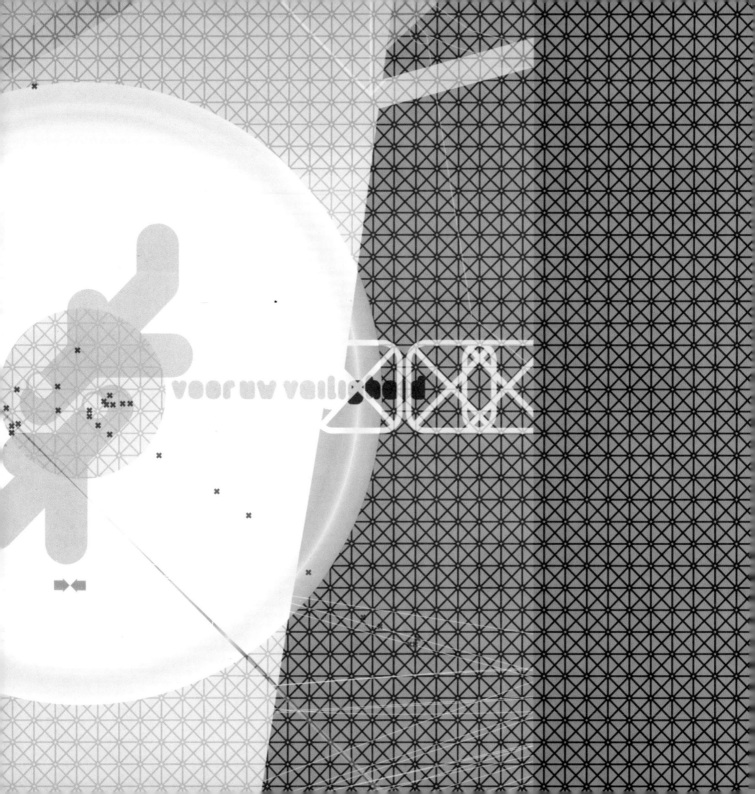

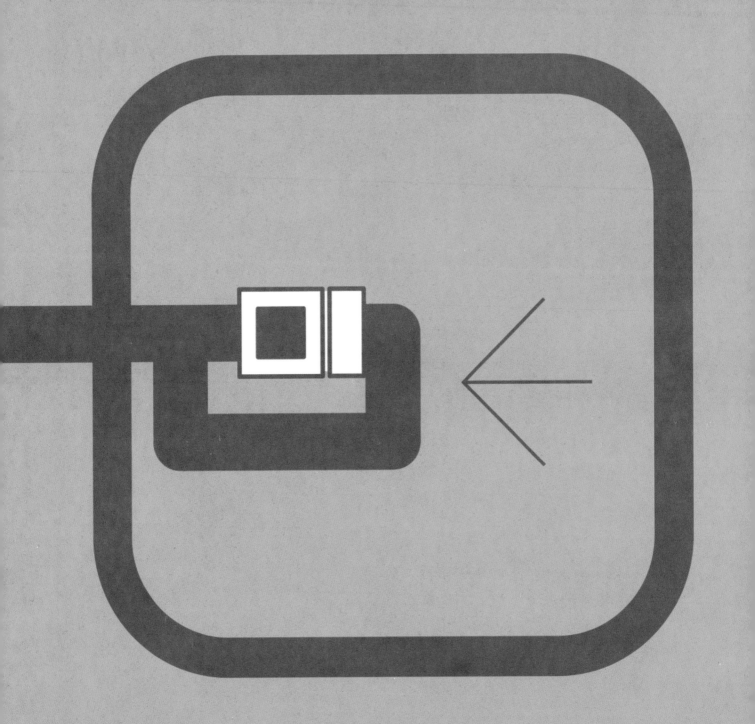

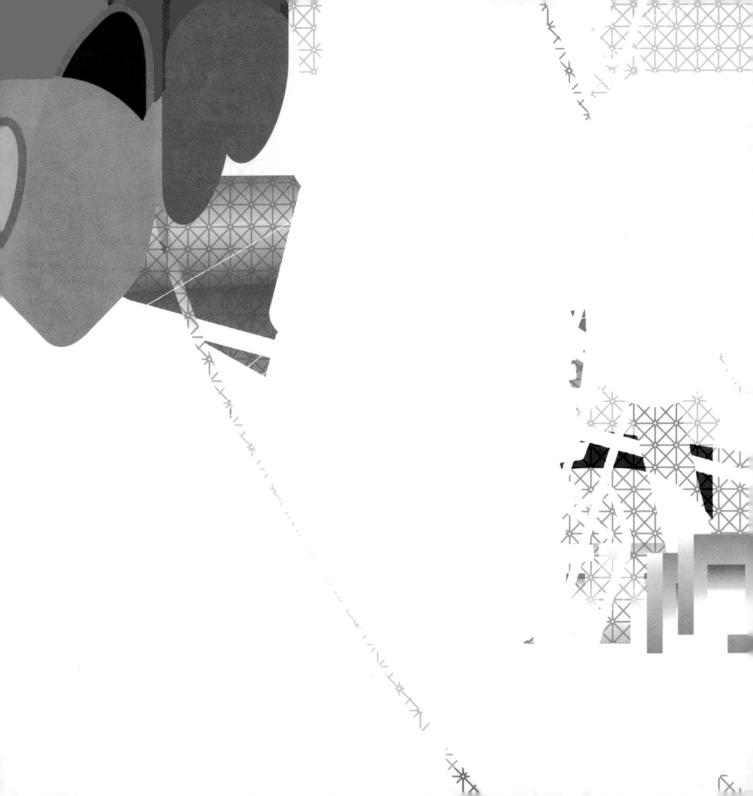

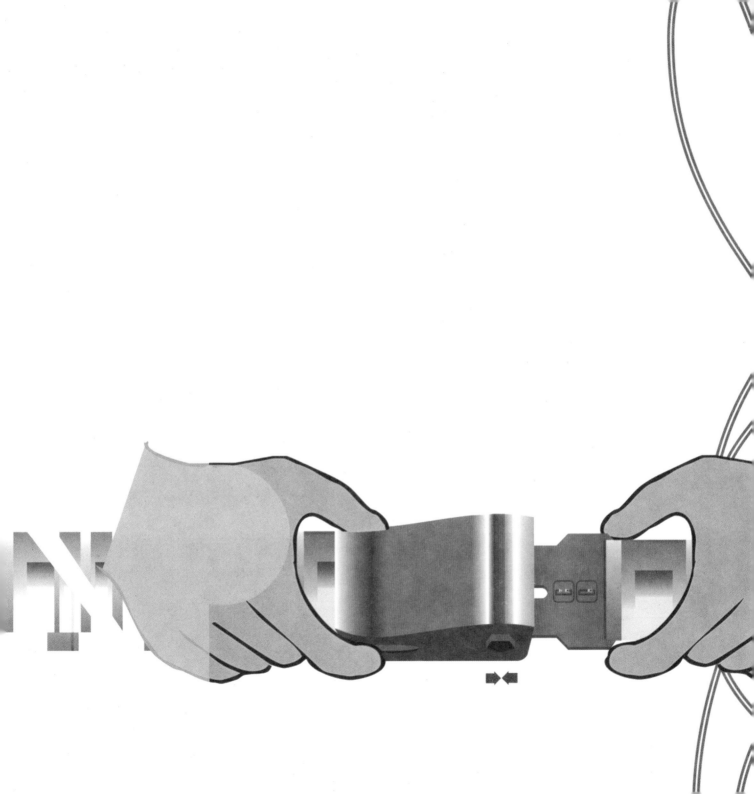

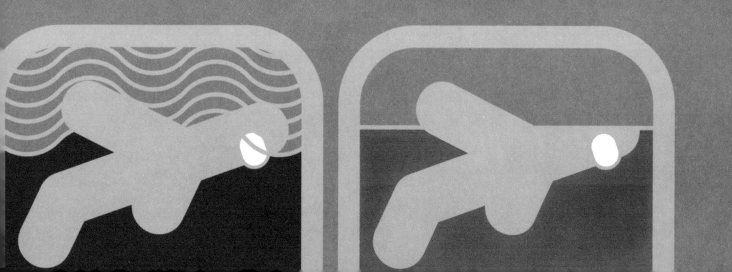

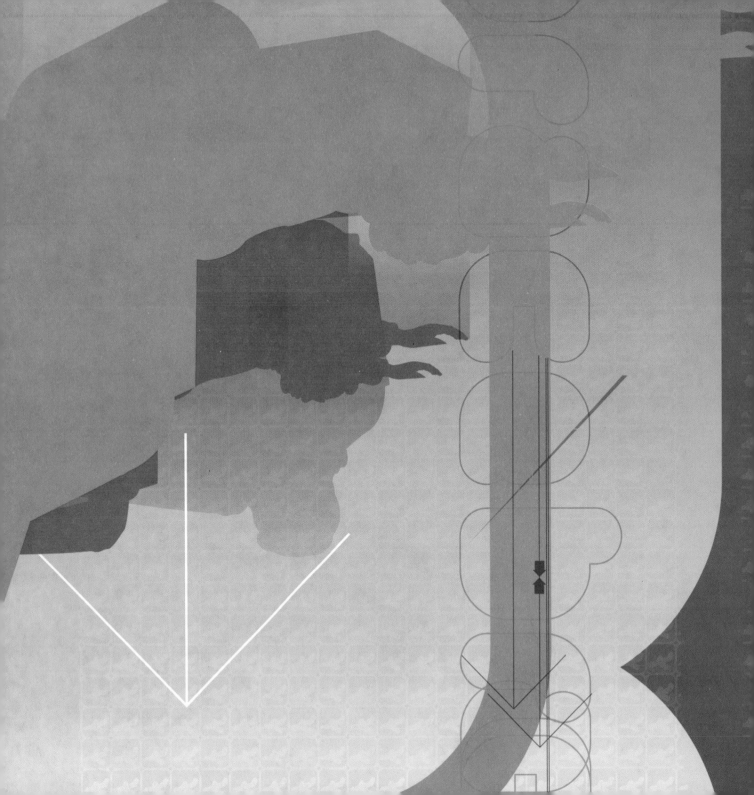

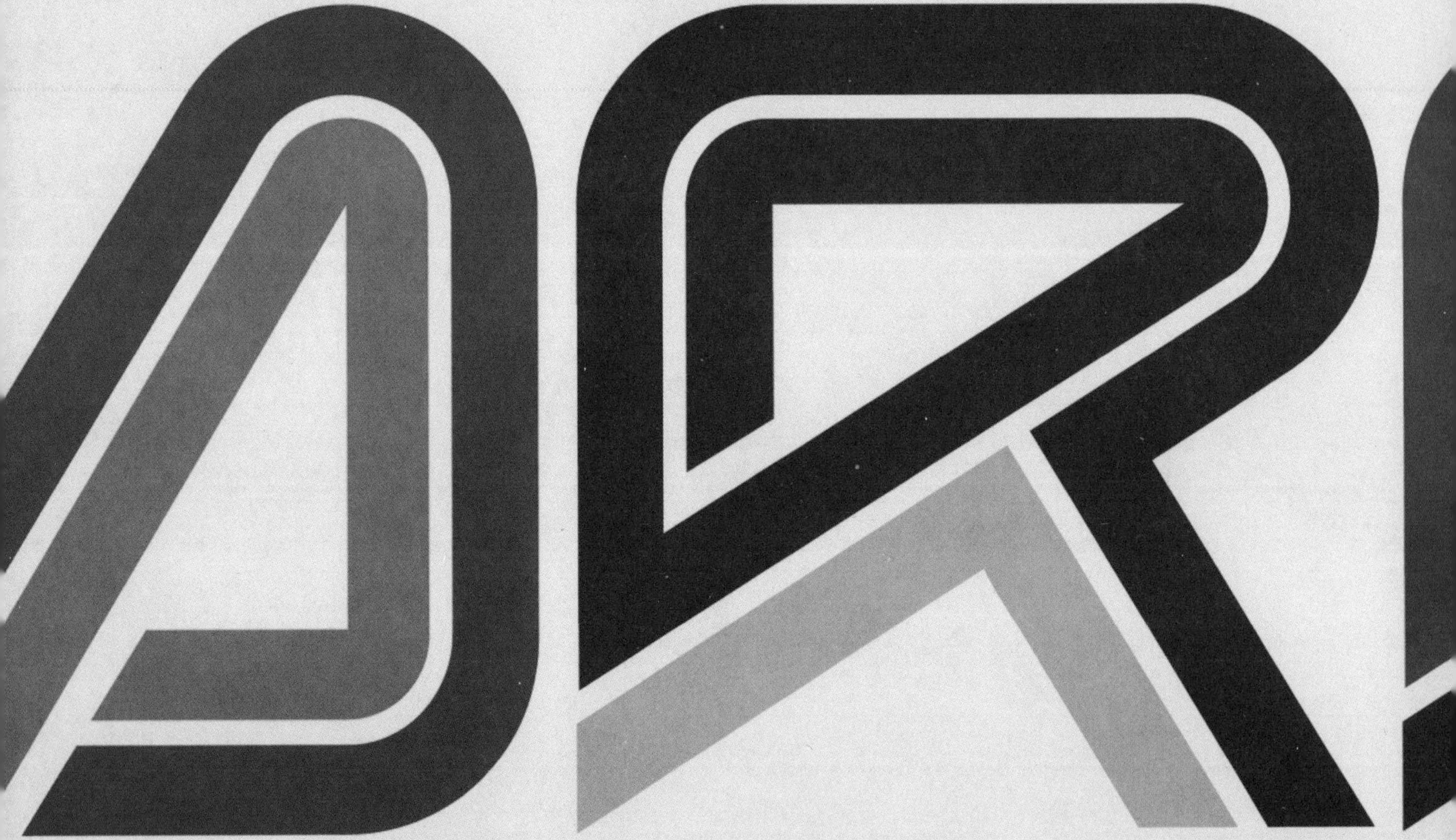

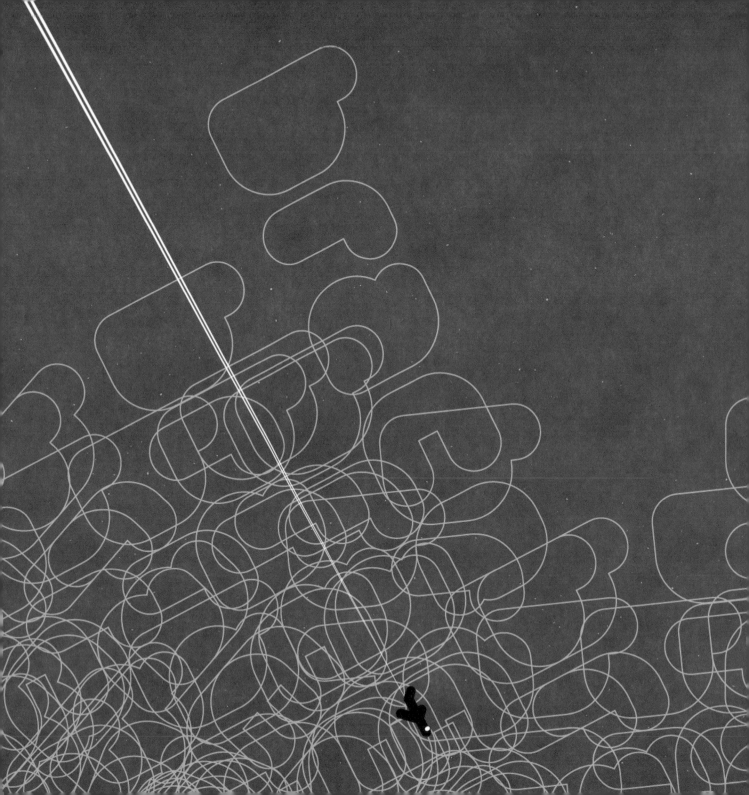

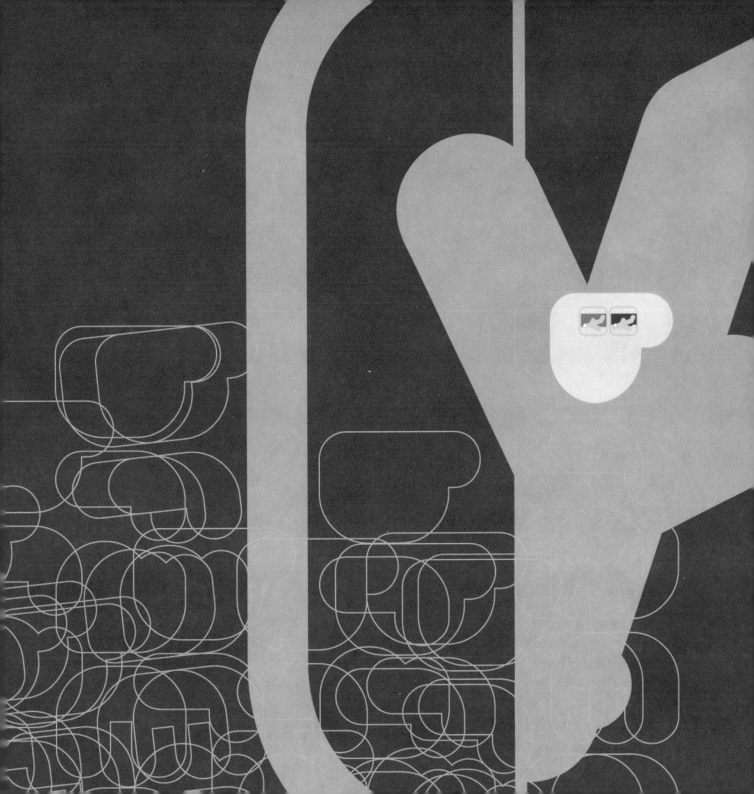

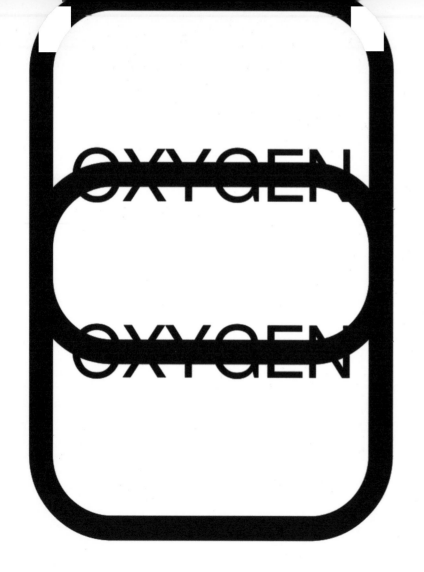

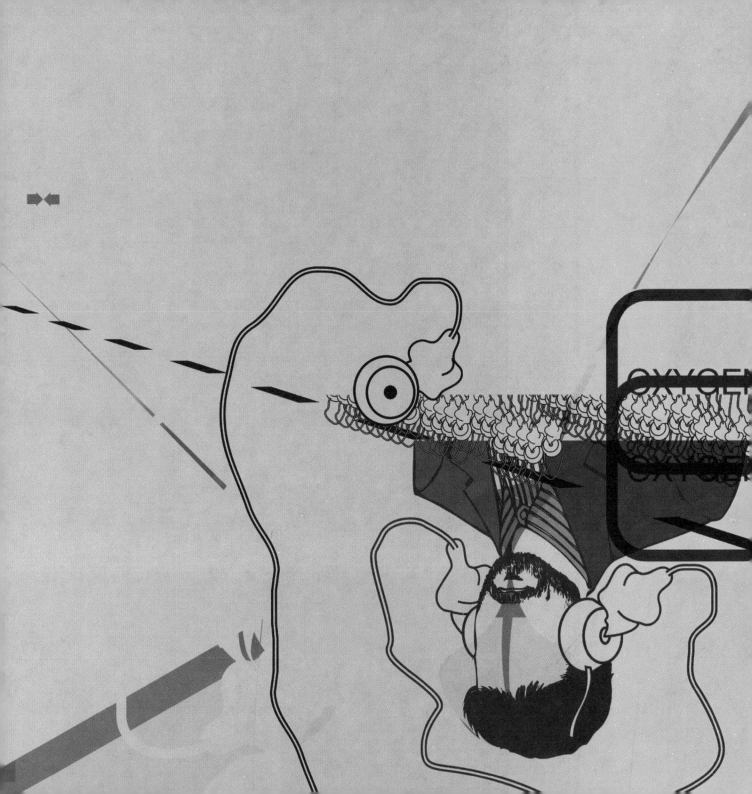

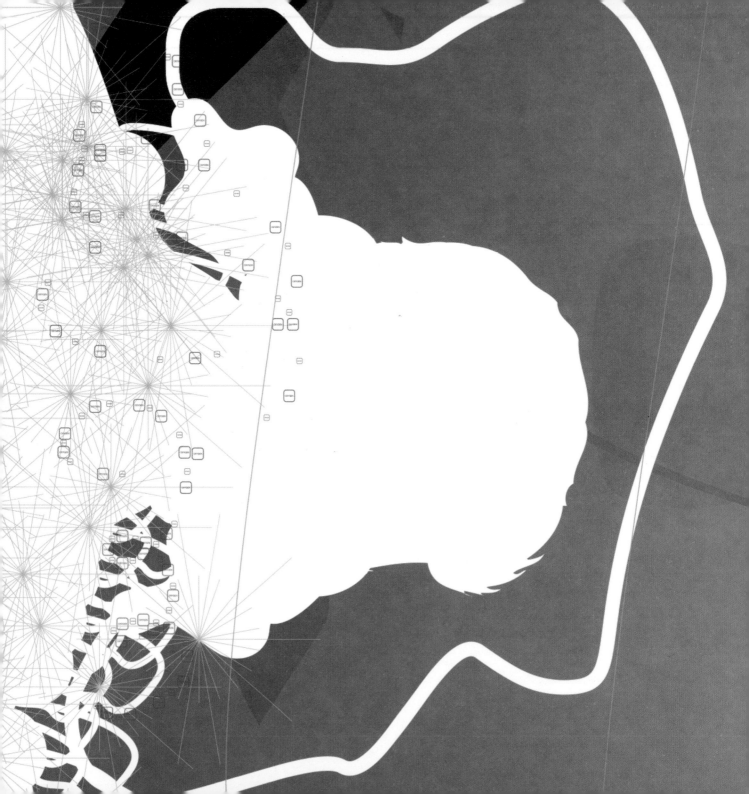

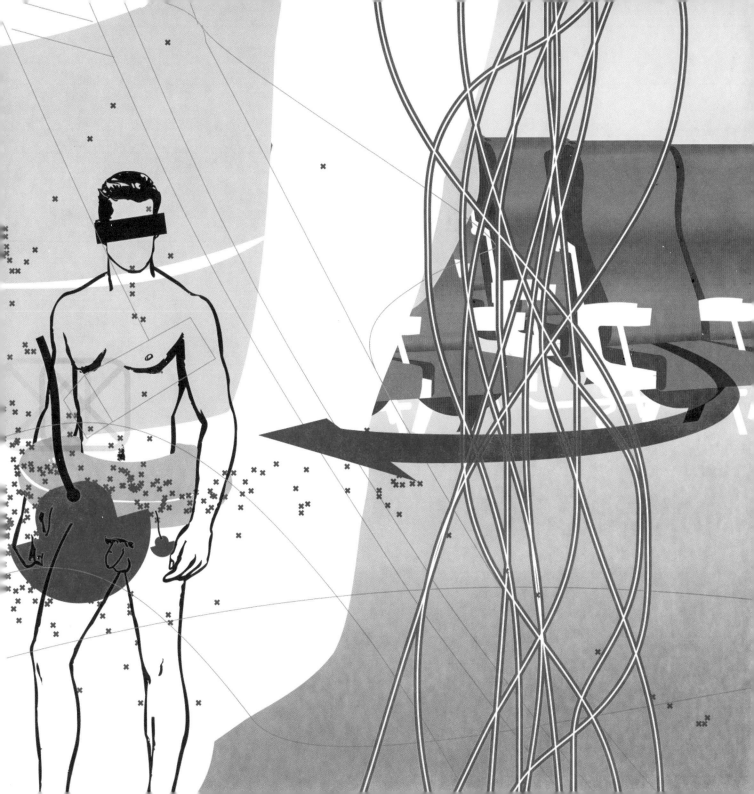

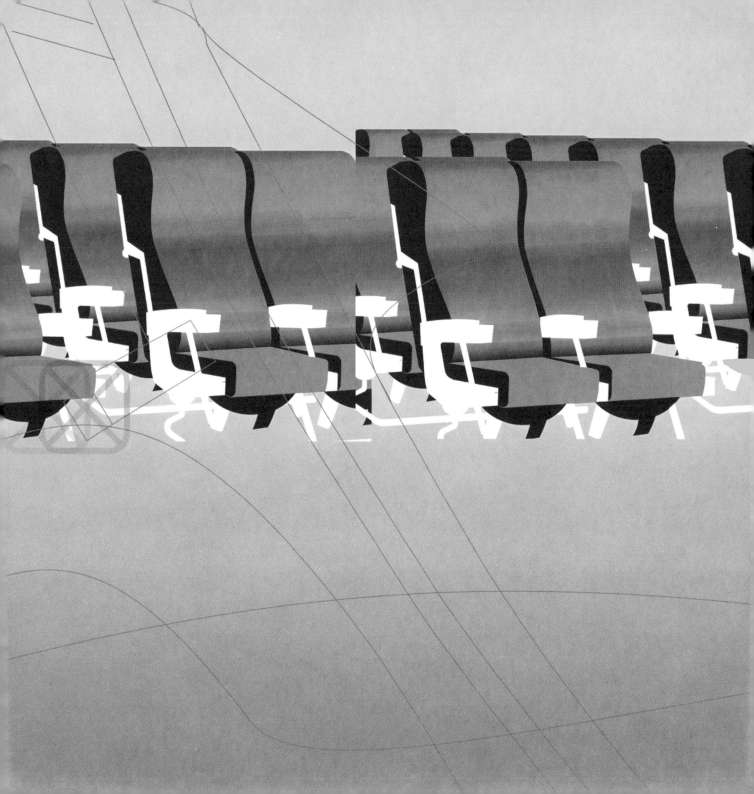

Northampton College
Library

654475	D	£12.95
741.6		

DO NOT INFLATE
✗✗ AS THIS MAY IMPEDED YOUR EXIT ✗✗
DED ASSOCIATES (DAUGHTRY, NIK; DAUGHTRY, JON)

BIG UP:
THANKS TO ALL THOSE AT LAURENCE KING PUBLISHING WHO MADE THIS PROJECT POSSIBLE
AND TO MICHAEL EVAMY AND MARC (@MAGMA). SPECIAL THANKS TO ALL THOSE AT DED,
WITH LOVE AND RESPECT TO EM AND NATTY.